BECAUSE OF THE CROSS

POEMS INSPIRED BY GOD

BECAUSE OF THE
CROSS

RON BROWN

TATE PUBLISHING
AND ENTERPRISES, LLC

Because of the CROSS
Copyright © 2015 by Ron Brown. All rights reserved.

No part of this publication may be reproduced, stored in a retrieval system or transmitted in any way by any means, electronic, mechanical, photocopy, recording or otherwise without the prior permission of the author except as provided by USA copyright law.

Scripture quotations are taken from the *Holy Bible, King James Version, Cambridge, 1769*. Used by permission. All rights reserved.

This novel is a work of fiction. Names, descriptions, entities, and incidents included in the story are products of the author's imagination. Any resemblance to actual persons, events, and entities is entirely coincidental.

The opinions expressed by the author are not necessarily those of Tate Publishing, LLC.

Published by Tate Publishing & Enterprises, LLC
127 E. Trade Center Terrace | Mustang, Oklahoma 73064 USA
1.888.361.9473 | www.tatepublishing.com

Tate Publishing is committed to excellence in the publishing industry. The company reflects the philosophy established by the founders, based on Psalm 68:11,
"The Lord gave the word and great was the company of those who published it."

Book design copyright © 2015 by Tate Publishing, LLC. All rights reserved.
Cover design by Junriel Boquecosa
Interior design by Gram Telen

Published in the United States of America

ISBN: 978-1-68028-334-1
Poetry / Subjects & Themes / Inspirational & Religious
15.03.03

I dedicate this book to the glory of God and to three of the most important people of my life:

To my wife, LaFon, whom I loved for over fifty years. LaFon's spirit is now in heaven, but the memories of her from those who knew and loved her will never fade. Also, to my gifts from God, my two children, Fonda and Randy. They are my inspiration and support.

Acknowledgment

I thank my dear friend, Shirley Depew, for her support. She is a dedicated community prayer warrior. I have known her and her husband, Ralph, for many years. Shirley is a teacher in our local school and provided me the proofreading I needed plus the prayers and inspiration that kept me writing.

Contents

Introduction 13

Part One: The Cross 17
    The Power of the Cross 19
    The Blood of Jesus 21
    The King of the Jews 23
    Victory at the Cross 25
    The Follower 27

Part Two: Troubled 31
    God Will Have a Way 33
    Lonely 35
    He Is Always There 36
    When You Need a Friend 38
    Christ Came to Me 40
    Follow Me 42
    My Life Has Changed 44
    Knocking at Your Door 46

Part Three: Prayer and Praise 49
    My Prayer 51
    Blessed Be the Lord 52
    A Sinner's Prayer 54
    The Light 56
    Believe When You Pray 58

Faith 60
Be Still and Know He Is God 62
Our Prayer 64
I Am Forgiven 67

Part Four: Love and Comfort 69
God Is Love 71
I Never Left You 73
Scars of Healing 75
God's Promise 77
The Comforter 78
A Love Song 80
God's Word 82

Part Five: Thoughts 83
Hugs 85
Fingerprints 86
God's Garden 88
Blooms 90
His Peace 92
Storms of Life 94
Ask Forgiveness 96
The Tongue 98

Part Six: Thinking Back 101
Wasted Years 103
My Loved One 106
She Loved 107

God's Plan for You 108
Christmas Time 111
Old-Time Camp Meetings 113
The Fifty-First Anniversary 115

Part Seven: Special Days and Special People 117
Mother's Day Without Mom 119
Heavenly Father's Day 121
Grandmothers 123
Thanksgiving 125
LaFon 127
The Preacher Man 129
My Daughter 131

Part Eight: He Is the Reason 135
Do You Know the Reason? 137
Christmas 140
The Small Barn 143
Heavenly Party 146
What Does Christmas Mean to You? 148

Part Nine: That's All 151
The Warnings 153
America the Beautiful, Once Again 156
What Would You Do? 158
The End and Beginning 161

Introduction

In June 1957, just after I graduated from high school, my parents moved us to a farm west of Bentonville, Arkansas. On July 21, I met my future wife-to-be on a blind date. A year later, just after she graduated, we were married. She was seventeen, and I was eighteen, and both of us were madly in love.

We left soon after the reception and headed for my hometown of Perryton, Texas. I had been offered a job as a draftsman for a construction company. Sometime in 1959, my parents moved back to Perryton, and because of that I have always thought that the Lord had a hand in me meeting my wife, LaFon. We had both given our hearts to the Lord when we were young but over the years had grown away from him.

We had been married for fifty years, and all of our two-week vacations were spread out to enable us to visit her parents. We traveled more in 2008 than any time in our marriage. In May, we went to Vegas to see some shows, and then in June, we met all of our family in Hot Springs, Arkansas, to celebrate our anniversary. The mountains of Colorado saw us in August, and in September, we visited aunts in Wichita, Kansas.

October 4 was LaFon's three-day, fifty-year class reunion in Bentonville. Since we were close to her sister's place in Carthage, Missouri, we went with them to Branson.

We were home only two weeks when it happened. October 26 will always be a bad day. While going to look at the foliage at a local lake, I glanced off the road and hit a culvert. It tore the bottom of my pickup out from under me, and I was sitting on the ground. We both had bad injuries, but mine were more severe than hers. I was flown to Amarillo, and she was taken by ambulance. The doctors told my grandson that I might not live because my bladder was busted, and that if I did live—my left heel was shattered so badly—they might amputate my foot. But God reached down for me and told the doctors what they needed to do.

After they operated, they induced a coma that lasted ten days so the bladder could heal. All the bones were placed in the heel with hopes that they would mend together. Praise God they healed. I limped out of the hospital on crutches, three days before Christmas, and my daughter took me to Missouri to be with our family.

Because of the CROSS

While my wife was being treated, they found a small cancer in her lung. It was small enough they said special pills would take care of it. She was then released to her sister a week before Thanksgiving. In the accident, LaFon had also broken her right thumb, and since she was wheelchair bound for a while, her sister took her to Missouri to be with her.

Since we were both in Missouri, our children came there for Christmas. All of LaFon's family was together for what we didn't know would be her last Christmas. A few days into January, the pills arrived for her to start taking. Soon, she could not keep anything down and started dehydrating. We took her to the hospital where she was treated a few days and released. Three or four days later, we repeated it. This time they found the problem—stage four colon cancer, and it had spread to her liver. They said she had two months at the most. She did not feel sick or hurt anytime during our trips. She tried chemo but it made her even sicker, so she stopped.

Prayers were made by people in California and all the way to North Carolina, and from South Texas to North Dakota.

Cards of encouragement came in every day, *but* that wasn't God's plan. He knew she was going Home many days before we did any celebrating during our travels.

That's the reason we traveled as often as we did and got to see everyone that she wanted to see. That's why the family got to be together at Christmas. That's the reason I was healed, so I would write poems about His glory and love.

She graduated from this earth in April 2009. At her funeral, we celebrated her life by showing a video made by our children from scenes of the past fifty years. God gave us the peace and comfort that He promised, as we honored her graduation to the new life.

May God richly bless everyone that reads these poems, as He has blessed me while writing them. I pray that they will be an inspiration for you to draw closer to Him.

Part One: The Cross

The Power of the Cross

When all of God's Saints, from years gone by,
Killed innocent animals for their sacrifice;
The sacrifices were to atone for their sins,
And for this cause, the animal gave its life.

Just like the animal, the Lamb of God's Life
Was the supreme sacrifice;
He wiped the slate clean of our sins,
When on the Cross, He gave His life.

When the Lamb of God died on the Cross,
There was a lot of weeping at His crucifixion.
The Power of the Cross was just beginning;
God's promise was fulfilled with the Lamb's
Resurrection.

The Power of the Cross stopped all the weeping;
The Lamb of God arose from the dead.
With the Cross, God made a new covenant,
And He will always fulfill what He said.

The Cross is the object of our faith,
When through our faith we believe;

Our old mortal bodies are washed away,
And a new spiritual body we receive.

When we call upon the Power of the Cross,
And the promises God has given,
We are all children of the resurrection,
And will be with Him in Heaven.

Blessed be the name of the Lord,
Through the Cross, He gives us daily blessings.
I will praise His name with a song,
And magnify Him with thanksgiving.

The Power of the Cross will cover us,
When to Jesus we give our souls.
We have the promise of eternal life,
Because we know our God has control.

> Why do you seek the living among the dead?
> He is not here, but has risen!
>
> The Son of Man must be delivered into the
> Hands of sinful men, and be crucified, and
> The third day rise again.

Luke 24:5,6,7

The Blood of Jesus

As the crowds began to gather
Around a place called Golgotha hill,
There was a lot of yelling and disturbance,
But all of a sudden it became deathly still.

The sky became black with heavy clouds as
The earth beneath their feet began to shake!
Christ Jesus had taken His last earthly breath
As He said, "Father, I give you my life to take."

Some of the people standing around the cross,
Were followers of Him and His Word.
They all were weeping at His loss,
But had forgotten what they had heard.

For in three days, He would arise.
Death would be defeated that day.
He would ascend to His Father in the skies,
But His word with us would always stay.

While we were still bound by sin,
Christ died for us, on Calvary's tree.
We are justified by His blood and
Saved from the wrath that is to be.

Jesus put away sin by His sacrifice;
His blood has made us free.
The pain and suffering that He went through,
Was all done just for you and me.

His blood will wash us white as snow;
It does away with the penalty of sin.
The light of His glory in our lives,
Will shine when His love we have within.

When trials and temptations of this world,
Seem to get the best of you,
Just plead for the Blood of the Lamb,
Christ Jesus, our Savior, will see you through.

He redeemed us to God by His blood.
His blood washed away our many sins;
By His blood, we have a new covenant.
All that is needed is to ask Jesus to come in.

Jesus came to earth that we may have life.
He paid the sacrifice for you.
By the love and grace of the Father,
The gift of salvation is offered to you.

The King of the Jews

I saw my Lord from afar, kneel and begin to pray.
Close by, His friends began to sleep.
"Not My will but Thine be done,"
My Lord prayed and began to weep.

The stillness was shattered by a crowd,
As Judas quickly, pointed to my Lord.
They grabbed His arms and led Him away,
This gentle Man, that teaches God's Word.

The "King of the Jews" the crowd began to mock;
Laughs and jeers were heard everywhere.
It wasn't long before someone threw a rock,
And a soldier put some thorns in His hair.

The whips stung deep as they cut into His flesh,
Sweat and tears ran down His face.
They made Him pick up and carry His cross,
And after a distance, they said, "This is the place."

They made Him lay down on the cross,
Rusty spikes were driven into His hands.
This humble Man who was the Son of God,
Is giving His life and making His stand.

The blood Christ shed for us that day,
Was to cleanse our hearts from within.
Christ paid the price for all of us,
The price He paid was for our sins.

As Christ hung on the cross that day,
He looked to His Father above and cried,
"My spirit I give to you this day,"
Then He gave up the ghost and died.

Death couldn't hold Him in the ground,
On the third day He would arise.
One of these days He will come again,
On a cloud, floating in the skies.

And on the third day He shall arise.

Matthew 20:19

…And if I go and prepare a place for you,
I will come again and receive you unto myself.

John 14:3

Victory at the Cross

There is a war being fought in this world today
By Christians everywhere that believe on the cross.
It is a war against sin and the evil it holds;
We will win because there is victory in the cross.

When Christ chose us as one of His own,
And to Him we confessed our sins;
By His blood, shed on the cross, He forgave us,
And through Him, our new life begins.

We may be sad and overly downhearted
Before, we ask Him, to come into our life.
Now we have a smile and joy in our heart.
Because of the cross, a change came over our life.

We still fight against the way of the enemy;
We now have put on the armor of God.
It is an everyday battle that we will win,
Because Jesus is with us everywhere we trod.

As a soldier of God's army, we are expected to fight,
The sins that are taking over our nation.
It takes lots of prayer and persistence from us,
And the victory of the cross is our motivation.

When Christ bore stripes for our healing,
He gave His life on the cross for all to believe.
He rose the third day; He defeated death and sin,
And He offers the same to all that will receive.

Many are chosen by Him to receive;
Those that believe in Him, their souls are not lost.
Few are selected because many do not believe,
On the victory that comes with the cross.

The cross that Jesus was hung on to die,
Will always be a symbol of the fight against sin.
Jesus came to earth to die just for us,
Because of the victory of the cross, we win.

> He will swallow up death in victory.

> Isaiah 25:8

> Wherefore take unto you the whole armour
> Of God, that ye may be able to withstand
> In the evil day…

> Ephesians 6:13

The Follower

There were three of them sentenced to die,
Either by hanging or be crucified.
The soldiers had finished getting them ready
And people stared at them as they walked by.
Stripped almost of all of their clothing,
They begin to walk out of the cell.
The soldiers were told to guard them,
And to start walking when they heard the bell.

They were made to carry their own cross
Out of town and up a hill a little ways.
One of them had been severely beaten;
He was a young man in His thirties, I'd say.
The weight of the cross made Him stumble;
You could tell He was in great pain.
He carried the cross as far as He could,
And when He fell, His trying to get up was in vain.

The soldiers grabbed a man from the crowd.
"Help Him carry His cross" he was told.
The man helped the young man to His feet,
Picked up the cross and began up the road.
The soldiers continued to strike them,
As they struggled to carry their crosses up the hill.

Soon they were at the place of the crosses,
A place called Golgotha hill.

They nailed each of them to a cross;
The young man was second in line.
They put the young man between the other two,
And they raised the crosses, one at a time.
On the young man's cross they nailed a sign,
"King of the Jews," I heard them say.
I looked at the young man hanging there;
What a tragedy was committed that day!

The young man, "King of the Jews," had done no wrong.
The other two deserved to die.
Above all the noise and cheers from the crowd,
I could hear them holler, "Crucify."
The other men began to moan and scream,
As their bodies, became wracked with pain.
But from the young man, little was heard.
Huge tears ran down his face as He suffered the pain.

"Who is this man that seems so meek?"
I asked the man next to me; I really wanted to know!
That man is Jesus, our Savior and Lord,
The King of the Jews, I was surprisingly told;
The man was a follower of Jesus Christ and
He told me of the good deeds Jesus had done,

Why He was being crucified on the cross and
That He was God's Beloved Son.

"My God, My God, why have You forsaken me,"
The young man Jesus began to cry.
Clouds of darkness began to cover the land;
The earth shook and thunder shattered the sky.
At that moment I asked the follower,
"How could I become one of them?"
The follower said I must repent of my sins,
Ask forgiveness and pledge my life to Him.

How could I be a follower of the Lord Jesus,
When He was dying on the cross?
I wanted to be a follower but,
Jesus dying, would be the world's loss.
The follower, I think his name was John,
Explained to me the best he could,
How to give my life to Christ,
And to do all the things I should.

I looked again at "The King of the Jews,"
Tears begin to roll as I cried.
I heard Him say "It is finished,"
As a soldier put a spear in His side.
Christ Jesus was taken down from the cross,
And laid in a tomb just down the road.

Jesus was such a gentle person
And loved everyone He met, I am told.

I became a follower of Christ Jesus that day,
And in three days good news was heard;
Christ Jesus had risen and defeated the grave;
Jesus had been true to His word.
After hearing that Jesus had risen,
I began to earnestly spread His word.
I told everyone how I had been saved,
And about the risen miracle that had occurred.
How He had come to earth to save the world;

He gave victory to those that were sick and lame.
He went about the land doing miracles,
But He did not want fortune or fame.
Our Jesus Christ was a humble man;
The books of the Bible record His deeds.
He definitely is that same person still
And you can pray to Him for your needs.

The redeeming blood He shed that day
Was shed on the cross for me, and for you.
Will you pick up His cross and help carry the load?
If you will, you will be a follower too.

> And he who does not take up his cross and follow
> after Me, is not worthy of Me

Matt 10:38

Part Two: Troubled

TROUBLED!

TROUBLED!

TROUBLED!

TROUBLED!

TROUBLED!

TROUBLED!

TROUBLED!

When you have Jesus in your life,
Your troubles seem to shrink.

God Will Have a Way

When you feel that your life has been wasted
And all hope seems to be slipping away...
No matter how dark the skies may look
And when it looks like there is no other way,
God will always have a way.

Your troubles may seem to build every day;
Your faith, which was strong, but now is weak.
You feel like you are alone in this world;
You are easy to anger and fast to speak,
But God will have for you a way.

When you put your trust in God to lead your life,
Your trials will become less filled by sorrow.
Insurmountable trials will vanish,
If you trust in Him for your tomorrow.
Your God will have a way.

You may have given your heart to God
Many years ago, and have now gone astray.
You realize you have not been true to Him,
And are not following His ways
But, God can bring you back to His way.

He'll put joy unspeakable in your heart;
His peace will fill the void that is there.
When you pray to our Lord and Savior,
He will lighten your load and make your days fair.
He will always have a way.

The road to Heaven is straight and narrow.
Can you imagine what Heaven will be?
The angelic choruses will be singing of His glory,
And all the saints you will get to see.
When Jesus died on the cross for us,
By His blood, He made the way.

> Behold, I send my messenger before thy face,
> Which shall prepare thy way before thee.

Matthew 11:10

Lonely

I'm a very lonely person today;
My loved one has passed away.
I would be more than lonely today,
But God's love is with me to stay.

The tears I shed, the prayers I made
While by my loved one's side,
Please send down your healing power,
Dear Lord, help us I cried!

God heard our prayers…sent down His love,
But her healing wasn't meant to be.
Our loved one was going Home with Him…
God has sent His Comforter to me.

The loneliness will soon go away, and
The memories of her will linger on.
God leads me through my life each day…
His tender mercy, I depend on.

> And I will pray to the Father, and He shall
> Give you another Comforter that he may abide
> With you forever.

John 14:16

He Is Always There

When your whole world seems to crumble,
And starts to fall in around you.
Just keep your trust in Jesus because,
He knows what you're going through.

We often wonder why things happen;
There seems to be two seasons in your life:
One that gives us plenty and joy;
The other one gives us sorrow and strife.

God said our Christian life would not be easy.
He said there would be lots of burdens to bear.
But if we pray and believe in Him,
He said He would always be there.

We must go through the trials unafraid,
But sometimes we feel He has left our side.
The Lord's abundant love was shown to us,
When He hung on the cross and died.

Because of the CROSS

The season of sorrow is a test of our faith,
When, we seem to grow closer to the Lord.
We humble ourselves and pray more to Him,
And always study more of His Word.

God hears our prayers and wipes away our tears.
He wants us to be of good cheer.
The lesson He taught us will strengthen us
Because He said, "I'll always be here."

> For He himself said,
> "I will never leave you nor forsake you."

Hebrews 13:15

When You Need a Friend

If your world is collapsing around you
And you really don't know what to do;
Everyone is so busy with their lives,
They don't want anything to do with you.

That's when a true friend shows up for you;
Friends that are always there, and will never relent.
What better friend is there but the Lord, and
His helping hand is with you, when from sin you repent.

Maybe you have lived a fast and furious life;
It was probably one that you could not afford.
Now that your life's troubles have increased,
Where can you go but to the Lord?

When you start searching for comfort to your soul,
And a refuge in the time of a storm,
Your friend and Savior will hear your plea,
When to His wishes, your life you conform.

When you need a friend, someone you can depend on;
The Lord is never very far from you.
When was the last time you fell on your knees,
And asked Him, "Lord, what should I do?"

Because of the CROSS

Maybe at one time, you knew this friend
But over the years, you have drifted away.
You have quit putting your trust in Him,
And started doing all things, your way.

It's time to ask your friend to come back,
Although the Lord never left, it was you;
He has been there all the time waiting,
And you have failed to seek Him, in what to do.

Just remember that He is a forgiving God,
And He loves to hear praises and prayers from you.
No matter how far in sin you have been,
His grace will offer salvation to you.

Continue to have faith in our Lord;
Trust Him in everything you do.
Always give Him thanks for what you have,
And His mercy and grace will be extended to you.

> Let thine heart retain my words;
> Keep my Commandments and live.

Proverbs 4:4

> A friend loveth at all times.

Proverbs 17:17

Christ Came to Me

When I was a hopelessly lost sinner
And nothing but trouble could I see.
I had decided to take my life,
But that's when Christ came to me.

He told me not to take my life;
I was too important to Him.
He said a new life for me was just beginning,
And He needed me to work for Him.

He told me to confess my sins,
And He would remember them no more.
I needed to read and study His Word,
And I would have blessings as never before.

I would be led to faraway places.
I was to tell His story and read His Word.
Places I have never been needed His salvation.
Places where never before, God's Word was heard.

Because of the CROSS

My life now is very satisfied:
I spread His word as often as I can.
The joy that He brings to my life
Keeps growing greater according to His plan.

Eternal life is my destination;
The streets of gold I now see.
The life that I had given up on,
Was now blessed because Christ came to me.

Follow Me

Jesus said, "Just follow Me,
And believe what I say and do.
Follow Me, just follow Me,
And I will always be there for you."

When sickness and trials get heavy,
And you don't know what you should do.
Just remember to follow Jesus,
With His love, He covers you.

Though your prayers just seem to vanish,
And your hope is growing dim;
Just put your faith in Jesus,
And follow, follow Him.

The songs of praise and prayers you make,
To our Father in Heaven above,
Are heard by Him and cherished by Him,
And He will fill you with His love.

Because of the CROSS

So, don't despair and feel all alone,
Because Jesus is still by your side.
Just one more prayer and follow Him;
His love in you abides.

By prayer and faith you will be healed,
All sickness will fade, all trials will leave, and
When you follow Jesus and with faith you pray,
Jesus will hear you, because you believed.

My Life Has Changed

For many years I have struggled,
But somehow I made it through.
All because of the presence,
Of a Savior I never knew.

My life was in such turmoil,
And nothing I did seemed right.
I walked many years in darkness,
Until, Jesus showed me the light.

"All you would need to have done,
Was to call upon my name.
I was here yesterday and today for you,
And I will always be the same."

Serenity has now entered my life,
Since Jesus came to me.
By His blood I have been cleansed,
And from sin He set me free.

A change in my life has been made;
Gone are the memories of my past,
With the love of Jesus in my heart,
I now have abundant peace at last.

Because of the CROSS

I have surrendered my life to Him;
I trust in His Holy Word.
I shall always praise His name,
And make sure His message is heard.

You also, can ask for His forgiveness;
He's patiently waiting for you to ask.
Jesus will shower you with His blessings.
And what He is asking is not a big task.

When your trials become overwhelming,
There is one thing that you can do.
Pray to your Heavenly Father,
Because, His Son is shining down on you.

Life will never be without trials;
God's mercy and love will see you through.
Have faith in what His word says and
His strength, your spirit will renew.

God doesn't want anyone to perish,
But to have eternal life in His Heaven.
Those that don't believe His word,
Will spend eternal life in Satan's heaven.

Knocking at Your Door

There is someone who is knocking at your door.
Will you choose to let Him in or will you choose to ignore?
He is patiently waiting for you to decide,
Won't you open up your heart and let Jesus inside?

Yes, Jesus is the one that is knocking at your door.
Will choose to let Him in or will you choose to ignore?
He is patiently waiting for you to decide,
Won't you open up your heart and let Jesus inside?

My Lord and Savior really cares for you today.
Won't you open your door and ask Jesus in to stay?
When you confess your sins, Jesus will come into your heart,
He'll take your hand and lead your way from the start.

Yes, Jesus is the one that is knocking at your door.
Will you choose to let Him in or will you choose to ignore?
He is patently waiting for you to decide,
Won't you open up your heart and let Jesus inside?

Because of the CROSS

When you asked Jesus Christ to forgive you of your sins,
The love of God will change you completely within.
There is an abundant joy that will linger in your heart,
Because you know from His love you'll never depart.

Yes, Jesus is the one that is waiting at your door.
Please invite Him to come in and please don't ignore.
He is patiently waiting for you to decide.
Just open your heart's door and let Jesus inside.

Part Three: Prayer and Praise

PRAYER
AND
PRAISE

My Prayer

Dear Jesus, I pray that You will show me the way.
May I walk in Your footsteps each and every day.

May I never look back or to the left or right.
May I serve You completely with all of my might.

Lord, help me be a blessing to someone today.
May I help a lost soul that has gone astray.

Help me pray for the sick and care for the old.
May I help bring someone in from the cold.

Let me provide for the hungry and
run errands for the lame.
Let me do all these things Lord, in Your precious name.

Lord, may Your bountiful blessings come down on me.
May I share Your blessings with someone in need.

I am Your servant Lord, please hear my plea.
I pray to You, Jesus, draw me closer to thee.

AMEN

Blessed Be the Lord

Lord, the wants of my body are for Your Words.
It is filled with hunger every day.
The knowledge that Your Word provides me,
Directs my life's plan and leads my way.

My heart cries out for Your abundant love.
The love Your Son showed when He died on the cross,
And the blood He shed, that covered all of my sins,
Proved His love for me that I would not be lost.

My soul longs for a covering of Your grace;
It sings praises to Your glorious name.
Blessed be the Lord of Hosts, the God on High,
And the Spirit that dwells within me, who took
Away my shame.

The flood of darkness that covered my soul,
 Has been dissipated, by the Light of the Lamb.
My days are filled with so much joy because,
In my heart, I know the great "I AM."

Because of the CROSS

May you continue to shower me with Your blessings,
May I always be singing a song;
"Hallelujah," a great song of praise,
And I'll sing to Him, to whom I belong.

I thank you, O Lord, for Your loving kindness.
Your mercy has been more than I deserve.
I pray and honor You on this day,
May You always be the one I serve.

A Sinner's Prayer

Lord, you are a Shepherd I do not know.
My wants of this world are great;
My green pasture and still waters are
Never calm, but are always full of turbulence.
My soul is always searching, and
It leads me onto the path of evil.

I walk the valley with fear in my heart,
For my enemies are everywhere.
I do not have You to comfort or protect me.
What I have, I guard because I am selfish.
Because my cup of life always needs filled,
My life is never satisfied.

Lord, I confess my sins now to You,
And ask You to be my Shepherd.
Give peace to my life and lead me,
On the paths that You walk.
Help me fear nothing except You
And also be a comfort to my soul.

Because of the CROSS

Let my cup be filled with righteousness
And may Your mercy cover me;
Let me dwell in Your house forever.
I pray to You and ask these things today.

AMEN

The Light

The dominion of sin had covered my life;
I did not know the light of God's word.
I began to suffer an inner grief,
And I had no one to go to, but to the Lord.

I began to pray, Lord, hear my voice, hear my plea;
I have sinned and ask for your forgiveness.
The darkness of sin began to fade,
And He surrounded me with His loving kindness.

He forgave me of all my sins,
And He cleansed my life that very day.
God's saving light began to show,
As He, started leading my way.

Jesus is the light of the world;
In Him I will find no darkness.
The blessings that He gives to me daily,
Come from His unending goodness.

Because of the CROSS

When we give our hearts to the Lord,
A new life for us will begin.
The darkness of sin will shatter,
Because the light of the Lamb is within.

> The Lord is my light and salvation; whom
> Shall I fear?

Psalms 27:1

Believe When You Pray

When the burdens of life overwhelm you
And it seems more than you can bear.
Just turn your eyes upon Jesus,
Your burdens He will share.

If your body is full of sickness
And also racked with pain,
Just pray to the Heavenly Father;
You have nothing to lose, and everything to gain.

Jesus will help bear your sorrows,
When you pray with faith and believe.
God will heal the pain and
His healing you will receive.

The power of God will flow through you;
The evil one will have to leave.
Your body is a temple of the Lord
Because when you pray, you believe.

Because of the CROSS

Give praises to the Lord above
For a victory has been won.
Your prayers have been answered
By Jehovah, the Almighty One.

> Therefore I say unto you, whatever things you ask
> When you pray, believe that you receive them, and
> You will have them.

Mark 11:24

Faith

While prayer may be the key to Heaven,
It takes your faith to help open the door.
When you pray with faith to our Father,
His mercy and blessings you'll receive evermore.

Faith does not have to be in huge amounts;
It can be as small as a mustard seed.
It's how you use the faith in your heart,
That's when God will supply all your needs.

By grace through faith you are saved;
Faith is what Peter had while in prison.
The chains were loosed and the gates opened,
And by that same faith, we know our Lord has risen.

Faith is something you can have but not see;
It is something we use every day.
We get into our cars to go to the store,
Turn the key on, and expect it to start right away.

Because of the CROSS

Just like our cars, it takes a key
To start things in Heaven when we pray.
How we pray and believe in our heart
Will open the doors to Heaven, today.

Have faith in our Heavenly Father,
That what we pray for, we will receive.
He will hear and answer our pleas;
We must have faith in Him and believe.

Be Still and Know He Is God

Have you ever been in a situation
Where you wanted to say something,
But deep down something tells you
To hold your tongue and say nothing?

Have you ever wanted to eat something
So badly you could almost taste it?
Then something began to happen,
And you knew that you shouldn't do it?

Have you ever started to buy a car,
But something about it just wasn't right?
So you told the car salesman that
You had to sleep on it overnight.

Have you ever stopped to think
Why things like this often happen?
It may be the small voice of the Lord,
And sometimes you forget to listen.

We sometimes ask God for things,
But it is always that we need them now.
We are never still enough to hear what He says;
We just expect it to be there somehow.

Because of the CROSS

If we would just be patient and still
And know that He is the Lord,
We could probably hear His answers
And He would remind us of His Word.

We think that sometimes God doesn't care
Because He doesn't answer our prayers.
All the static we have in our lives
Keeps us from hearing, but God is always there.

When we enter into our special place to pray
And we give Him praise while on our knees,
That small, still voice we're able to hear
Because God is answering and is very pleased.

> O Lord, thou art my God; I will exalt
> Thee. I will praise thy name…

Isaiah 25:1

Our Prayer

Heavenly Father, as we humbly pray to You today,
We offer all praise and glory to You.
We give thanks to You for our many blessings,
And all the things for us that You do.
We thank You for the years You have protected us
From those that tried to oppress our land.
You have led us through many trials and wars,
And with You, we have always made our stand.

We thank you for Your bountiful mercy,
That You have given to cover our land.
Your grace on us has been more than sufficient,
Because You have blessed us by Your hand.
While our enemies try to devour us,
By taking away our freedom and rights;
We shall always trust Your Word, Lord,
And continually pray to You day and night.

Our nation has turned its back to You.
They take no heed to read Your Word.
Some of the people that govern our world,
Not a word from Your book, have they ever heard.

Because of the CROSS

We, as a nation, have failed to honor You,
As we did when our nation first began.
Now You have looked the other way,
And in two thousand and one, our destruction began.

Although we have fasted and prayed,
And things we prayed for did not come,
We still put our trust and faith in You Lord.
You are still in control, our Lord, the Holy One.
Lord, we pray that You will put us in Your favor
And anoint us with Your mercy and grace.
Gather us back into Your arms again;
May we know that our God is in this place.

We pray Lord that You will forgive our nation
From the sinful things they have done.
We as Your servants, ask forgiveness
From our Lord and Savior, the Almighty One.
Help us take back the nation we love
By helping us with a great revival.
Put condemnation in the sinners heart
And the desire to understand Your Bible.

Help us be strong for Your chosen people.
May we be able to help them in their trials.
As a nation we must be their friend and be strong.
When they ask for help, there will be no denial.

Put our nation in the straight and narrow pathway;
Do not let us stumble or turn away.
May our nation return to serve only You,
And may it be that way until the last day.

We thank You Lord, for hearing our prayer.
May we walk in your light every day.
Continue to lead and bless our nation,
Heavenly Father, in this we ask, as we pray.

Blessed is the nation whose God is the Lord.

Psalm 33:12

I Am Forgiven

God's plan is on my mind today;
What does He have planned for me?
Am I doing His perfect will?
Am I trusting God's Plan for me?

I've been through troubled waters;
My stormy life was very fast.
Now I know Jesus, my Savior,
And He has forgiven me of my past.

Though storm clouds seem to gather,
They no longer frighten me.
The love and mercy of my Lord
Is abundant, and it is free!

Now my life is full of His blessings,
Since Jesus came to me.
I praise and worship at the feet
Of the one who died for me.

He tells me not to fear or worry;
Your joy, they will take away.
I need to keep His words in my heart,
And He will guide me every day.

Worrying will not lengthen your life,
Nor will it supply any of your needs.
The goodness of God will set aside your worries.
By your faith in Him, He will bless your seed.

Although I sometimes stumble,
Jesus is there to pick me up.
He is my Shepherd, I shall not want,
Because He says, "Come drink of My cup."

His plan is on my mind today.
What does He have planned for you?
Are you letting Him lead the way?
God's plan should be on your mind too.

> Give thanks always for all things unto God
> and the Father in the name of our Lord
> Jesus Christ.

Ephesians 5:20

Part Four: Love and Comfort

LOVE
AND
COMFORT

God Is Love

Do you have Love in your life?
Do you know Love by knowing the word?
Life can be miserable without Love
But joy comes by the Word you have heard.

Love is an important part of life,
And our world was created by Love.
Life without Love can be very dark
But the Word gives light that comes from above.

When we have Love in our life,
We need to show Love to others.
Tell sinners about the Love you have,
And not just to our Christian Sisters and Brothers.

Happy is he that has Love in his heart,
For his days shall be filled with contentment.
Love will show mercy and kindness
To those that have made a commitment.

Love never has words of discouragement
But will always build you up higher.
Love is continually there for you
And can fill your heart's desire.

Love is attentive and caring;
It can also be demanding.
When Love is a dominate factor in your life,
You will have a greater understanding.

So, if you are troubled and deep in sin,
And never discovered the True Love,
Just call on Jesus, the Word you have heard,
With open arms HE will welcome you,
Because *God Is Love*.

> But God who is rich in mercy, because of His great
> love with which He loved you, even when we were
> dead in trespasses…

Ephesians 2:4–5

> God is love; and he that dwelleth in love,
> Dwelleth in God and God in him.

1 John 4:16

I Never Left You

There was a time in my life without Jesus,
I began to turn my back on Him.
When He would call my name,
I would hang my head in shame,
Because, I had turned my back on my Jesus.

The pleasures of life grew much brighter,
The farther I strayed from the Lord.
I knew my lifestyle was changing,
A change I could not afford.

The peace of the Lord had left me,
Life's burdens began to grow;
I had everything I wanted,
But contentment, I did not know.

The devil had tried to destroy me,
But Jesus was by my side.
He wrapped his arms around me,
And He said, "With thee I still abide."

Jesus saved me from the shadows of death,
And He healed my broken bones.
When I called out to the Lord above,
He said, "You were never left alone."

I prayed and prayed to Jesus,
"Lord, forgive me and take me back in."
He said, "I never left you, you left me."
Now I am back in his arms again.

"I will never leave you or forsake you."

Heb 13:5

Scars of Healing

From the time God gives us our first breath,
    Until the day we take our last,
We will have many aches and pains,
    And scratches from the past.

The scratches we get when we are small,
    All seem to fade away.
The pain we had from puppy love,
    Went away the very next day.

The pain God felt when He watched his Son,
    Give His life on the cross, that day,
Is the same pain that He feels for us
    When we leave Him, and go astray.

Though pains very seldom leave a scar
    And aches can be relieved,
The scars of life we give to Him
    When we trust Him and believe.

Scars are a sign of God's healing,
    Though the wound may be very deep.
Like the scar of losing a loved one,
    When we send them to God to keep.

Ron Brown

The scars that were on Jesus' hands,
    Show that He really cares for you.
Scars are a sign of God's healing,
    From the hurt you have gone through.

> Blessed be the Lord, because He hath heard
> The voice of my supplications.

Psalms 28:6

God's Promise

When the one you love passes away,
　　There is an empty place in your heart.
The love you had for each other;
　　You swore you would never part.

Your earthly dreams are shattered,
　　And heartaches come your way,
But just remember what Jesus said;
　　He's in your life to stay.

He said He would always be with you,
　　And never let you go.
The agape love He has for you,
　　Is far greater than you will ever know.

God sends His Comforter down to you,
　　And with joy He fills your heart.
One of these days you'll see them again…
　　This time you will never part.

> Blessed be the God and Father of our Lord
> Jesus Christ, the Father of mercies and God
> Of all comfort, who comforts us in all our
> Tribulations.

2 Cor. 1:3,4

The Comforter

The loss of a loved one can test your faith
And cause you to doubt God's word.
God has said the way would not be easy;
Pray and hold on to Jesus, our Lord.

He will extend down His hand to you.
His love for you shall prevail.
He will heal the scars of death for you
Like the scars He healed from the nails.

God will send to you His Comforter;
It will dwell deep in your heart.
Your prayers will be answered,
And from you, He'll never depart.

Your loved one, God will carry away
To His heaven beyond the stars, and
The peace that He will give to you,
Will take away all of the scars.

Because of the CROSS

When the Comforter came, your faith was restored.
God proved your prayers had been heard.
The peace and joy you now have, is
That you believed in his word.

Prayer is the key to Heaven,
But it takes faith to unlock the door.
Pray to the Father every day, and
With faith, He'll love you more.

A Love Song

It's all about love; it's all about God's love.
It's all about God's wonderful love for you and me.
It's all about love; it's all about God's love.
It's all about God's wonderful love that set us free.

God gave His Only Begotten Son
To die on Calvary.
Christ shed His life's blood on the cross,
And from sin He set us free.

The pain He suffered while on the cross,
And as His tears ran down His face,
The love of God was shown that day
When His Son died in our place.

Now Satan will try to destroy your lives,
But God will intervene.
He gives to us His amazing grace:
It's a power that is unseen.

Because of the CROSS

God's untiring love will come to us
And wipe the many tears away.
No matter how hard the trial may be,
He will be with you every day.

Let's sing about love, let's sing about God's love.
Let's sing about God's wonderful love for you and me.
Let's sing about love, let's sing about God's love.
Let's sing about God's wonderful love that set us free.

God's Word

When a loved one is dying
    And you're sitting by their bed,
God's word will give you comfort
    As you remember what it said.

For if we believe in our hearts,
    That Jesus died and rose again,
They also which sleep in Jesus,
    God will also bring with Him.

The Lord himself shall descend from Heaven,
    And the trumpets will be heard.
The dead in Christ shall rise again,
    According to God's word.

We are not afraid of the darkness of night;
    We are all children of the day,
Because Jesus is the precious light,
    The light that leads the way.

      In the beginning was the Word and the Word was
      With God and the Word was God.

John 1:1

Part Five: Thoughts

THOUGHTS
THOUGHTS
THOUGHTS
THOUGHTS
THOUGHTS
THOUGHTS
THOUGHTS
THOUGHTS

Hugs

Give someone a hug today,
　　Just to let them know you care.
Give a loved one a hug today,
　　Let them know you'll always be there.

Hugs are given with lots of joy,
　　And hugs can be given in sorrow.
Giving hugs may give someone a boost,
　　And you may need one tomorrow.

Hugs can make you feel good all day
　　Whether you give or receive.
Hugs are a show of caring and love,
　　And some burdens, it helps to relieve.

Not everyone likes a hugger;
　　They offer a stiff arm to you.
But remember, it is worth a try,
　　Because they may really want you to.

Someone needs a hug today.
　　Hugs are always free.
Someone needs a hug today,
　　And God is sending it through you and me.

Fingerprints

There are all kinds of fingerprints;
Most are left by your hands.
A fingerprint can be left by a smile,
And a laugh sometimes can.

Fingerprints tell who you are
And what you want to say.
A fingerprint smile that you give to someone,
Can mean for them, to have a good day.

When you leave your prints on someone's life,
That someone has been blessed.
The fingerprint of love that you left with them,
Makes you different from the rest.

Fingerprints can be left in anger,
Regrets, or with lots of love.
The fingerprints that are left with love,
God sends them down from the Heaven above.

Someone needed some love today;
That someone might have been me.
God knows the people that you have touched,
Because, your fingerprints He could see.

Because of the CROSS

Fingerprints of love can only be found,
In someone where God's love, abides.
The love of God will conquer all fears,
When you have asked Him to come inside.

So be careful of the prints you leave,
And ask God to lead the way.
Someone is in need of a fingerprint of love,
So leave yours with them today.

God's Garden

Our heart is like a beautiful garden;
What we plant in it is what will come up.
Make sure that the seed is good and not bad,
And our deeds are abundant and not corrupt.

Our bodies are a temple of God,
So He will help us sow the seed.
When we call upon his name,
Our hungry souls, He will feed.

The seed God helps us plant in our hearts
Will grow when we seek His perfect will.
We can expect the harvest to be great,
And all our prayers, He will fulfill.

We need to be an example of Christian life,
And continue to sow God's spiritual seed.
Let our lives reach out to others
By giving comfort to those in need.

The fruit of the garden is sweet,
And the harvest will always be good.
God's blessings will be multiplied for us
When we praise His name as we should.

Because of the CROSS

You are the caretakers of God's garden.
Don't let the tares start to grow.
When the evil one starts to tempt us,
The blood of Jesus will begin to show.

The blood of Jesus will cover our life.
God's garden will continue to grow.
Our spiritual seed will start to bloom,
Because of Jesus Christ, whom we know.

Blooms

God gives us flowers that bloom in the spring,
    And flowers that bloom in the fall.
The fragrance and beauty that they bring,
    Is a pleasure to us all.

God blooms us in the years of our youth,
    Like the flowers that bloom in the spring.
What we do with that bloom when we are young,
    Will give glory to our King.

Our body is like the stem of the flower,
    That holds the bloom together.
The winds may blow, the storms may rage,
    And the bloom will not last forever.

When God plants the flower in our hearts,
    By His grace our bodies will be strong.
God's love in us will begin to bloom,
    And in our heart will be his song.

Most of the flowers that bloom in the fall,
    Have a short time to show their glory,
And when we give to God our later years,
    We can still tell of His story.

Because of the CROSS

So glorify the Lord and give praises to his name,
    And the blooms will continue to show.
Our life here on earth is very short,
    Then eternal life we will know.

God says to bloom where we are planted,
    Leaving His fragrance on life's way.
Then we'll bloom with Him forever,
    When God picks us for His bouquet.

His Peace

The meaning of peace to many people,
Is a quiet weekend at their home.
Some people find peace traveling many miles,
Admiring God's handiwork as they roam.

Our mind can give us a sort of peace,
While sitting by a babbling brook.
Others find peace in their backyards
By getting some rays or reading a book.

We must rely on our Heavenly Father,
To make our lives full of peace.
The Father knows just what we need, and
His grace and love for us will never cease.

It does not mean we will not have trials,
That we will face nearly every day.
His peace will enter our daily lives,
And our troubles seem to vanish when we pray.

Daily pitfalls and agitations will test our faith;
We will sometimes be quick to answer.
The peace of the Lord will see us through,
And our tongue, we will be able to conquer.

Because of the CROSS

While in sin, His peace you did not know.
You only found darkness as you looked for the light.
In desperation you called out to the Lord,
And His peace came to you, along with the light.

Jesus is the light of the world,
And for our sins He was crucified.
The joy and peace we receive from Him
Will keep our heart and soul satisfied.

When we have God's joy and peace in our hearts,
We will also have His understanding.
We can handle all the trials that come our way
And all the sacrifices that this world is demanding.

The blessings that will be given to us,
When we turn to God and believe,
By simply following the instructions in His word,
His amazing grace and abundant peace we will receive.

Peace I leave with you, My peace I give unto you.

John 14:27

"These things I have spoken to you, that in Me you may have peace. In the world you will have tribulation; but be of good cheer, I have overcome the world".

John 16:33

Storms of Life

There are times when storm clouds gather;
The storms of life will make us strong.
When we trust in the Lord, we can weather the storms.
By his word and our faith, we cannot go wrong.

The death of a spouse is a very strong storm;
We sometimes think God doesn't care.
God can easily heal a broken heart,
And He promised no more than we can bear.

We as Christians will have many storms;
Some are rarely noticed at all.
When the big storms hit and make us cry out,
That's when on God, we begin to call.

God knows storms will draw us closer to Him;
Our commitment to Him is put to the test.
He is never far from us and easy to find,
And in His arms we will find peace and rest.

It takes the storms to make us strong,
And we can find strength in His word.
The Lord rejoices in our prayers,
And every word of our prayers is heard.

Because of the CROSS

The wind may blow as the storm moves in,
And our faith will be shaken once more.
God is waiting to see what our actions will be.
When we trust in Him, our blessings He restores.

We know a Christian life is not easy.
It takes the storms of life to make us strong.
God's peace will bless our every move
So give Him praises in music and song.

God is good all through the storms.
His actions are not hit or miss.
God is continually standing by us.
Is your name on His eternal life list?

> Blessed be the lord, because he hath heard the
> Voice of my supplications.

> Psalms 28:6

Ask Forgiveness

In a world of wars and rumors of wars,
There is so much turmoil and unrest;
Storms and earthquakes are everywhere,
And our faith is being put to the test.

Storms have wiped out a lot of small towns,
Floods have covered and destroyed our land,
Our farmland has been in a drought,
And our leaders fail to take a stand.

We wonder why disease is so rampant;
Why our country is going downhill.
How come our economy doesn't get better?
There is a reason…we are going against
God's will.

God is not allowed in our schools,
And very few other public places;
We have taken God out of the picture,
And put into it, other faces.

Because of the CROSS

If America would ask for forgiveness;
If just all that believe would pray!
Our country would start coming out of the pit,
And it could happen this very day.

The Lord said if we humbly pray to Him,
And seek His favor again,
He would forgive and cleanse our sins,
And heal our land for us, once again.

The Tongue

The tongue can be a terrible weapon;
We carry it with us every day.
It's not the things we do that hurt;
It's usually what we say.

The tongue can kill a hopeful heart,
So think before you speak.
The Lord will direct the words you say,
If His guidance you will seek.

A tongue can build and it can tear down.
It depends on how you feel.
If God's love is in your heart,
You will always do His will.

A happy tongue does lots of good.
It spreads joy all around.
It's similar to a contagious laugh;
It can make a smile from a frown.

If you are feeling down and out
And your feelings you reveal,
Don't let the devil use your tongue…
Just pray to God… His love you will feel.

Because of the CROSS

Use your tongue for the glory of God:
Give praises to our king.
The grace that He will give to you,
Will cause your tongue to sing.

Whoso keepeth his mouth and his tongue,
Keepeth his soul from troubles.

Proverbs 21:23

Part Six: Thinking Back

THINKING
BACK
ALONG LIFE'S HIGHWAY

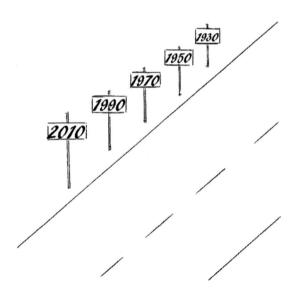

Wasted Years

As I look back on my younger years,
The things I did, the plans I made...
Makes me wonder where the time went,
And all those plans that began to fade.

While a teenager, I gave my life to Christ,
But wasn't told I would have to fight.
The evil one would always tempt me,
And some of my ways were not always right.

I forgot the Lord and did what I wanted,
But once in a while I would stop to pray.
I had turned my back on Him many times,
But somehow I knew He was with me to stay.

Then one day the Lord woke me up!
A wreck had almost cost me my life.
While in the hospital I began to pray,
Lord, help me and especially my wife.

The wasted years that I spent away from Him...
I begin to realize that He had not left me.
He would forgive me of my past sins
And would heal my bones and set me free.

There was a terrible blow to our family;
Advanced cancer was found in my wife.
It would raise its ugly head,
And soon it would begin to take her life.

We frantically called out to the Lord,
And lots of prayers, from friends, were given.
It wasn't what God had planned,
He took her spirit to be with Him in Heaven.

Those wasted years will always haunt me;
If I had served Him more, would she still be here?
Would God's plans been any different?
We will never know what He plans for us each year.

We just need to be still and know that He is God;
Study his word and listen for His call.
He has a reason for all our lives.
Christian or sinner, He dearly loves us all.

Because of the CROSS

Repent of your sins and turn your life over to Him.
He'll guide you through all your sorrows;
He will be with you through many trials,
And He is the same today and again tomorrow.

> I thought about my ways, and turned my feet to
> Your testimonies. I made haste, and did not delay
> To keep Your commandments
>
> Psalm 119:59,60

My Loved One

When God calls a loved one away,
The dreams of a family are shattered.
Jesus will still be leading the way;
God's plan is all that matters.

Our loved one's body was temporary;
Her spirit belonged to God.
God needed her spirit in Heaven,
So he gave our loved one, a nod.

She is now in Heaven and smiling,
The same smile, that was always on her face.
She is seeing all the wonders of Heaven,
Because she was saved, by God's amazing grace.

She is watching over us from above,
With smiles that only she could give.
While here on earth, she was filled with love,
That only a Mother can give.

We will miss her voice, her smile, and
The comment she made "Whatever."
We know we will meet again someday,
When we do, it will be forever.

She Loved

The song "She Loved" described my wife...
    Of the way she loved, and lived her life.
To her, a person was never ignored,
    And often her friends were really adored.

A welcoming smile would give you a clue;
    When you met her, she was happy to see you.
The love for her family everyone could see
    Because the joy in her heart, was pure and free.

God's love for us is much greater than my wife's,
    And it will extend into eternal life.
His grace is sufficient for all that believe;
    When we pray to God, his blessings we receive.

The reason my wife had so much love to give,
    Was she believed in God and that's the way she lived.
I give praise to the Lord for her terrific life;
    This beautiful lady He chose for my wife.

An excellent wife is the crown of her husband.

Proverbs 12:4

God's Plan for You

There are many things that will happen to us
As we travel along life's pathways.
If we have God in our hearts and doing his will,
He will direct us and show us the way.

My parents moved from Texas to Arkansas
While a lad, I still would be.
They didn't know they were doing God's will,
But they were doing God's will, for me.

Introduced by a friend, while on a blind date,
I met a young girl that would change my life.
God's plan for me was working again,
And a year later, she became my wife.

Lots of days and years have gone by
Since that day she said "I do."
We raised a terrific family through Him,
And God said, "That was part of my plan for you."

You see, I wasn't always there for God,
But He was always there for me.
He gave His son to die on the cross,
And He did it just for me.

Because of the CROSS

The Lord brings many special people into our life.
By His grace, He also takes them away.
It is a test that He gives us
To see how strong our faith is when we pray.

Sometimes things happen that we don't understand.
A special person to us was taken away.
Our dreams and hopes seemed shattered,
But God will never lead us astray.

A wife or a husband is a special person
That God's plan picked for you.
When He calls them Home, that's part of His plan.
But in His plan, He is still thinking of you.

Our lives will be forever changed;
God knows how much we loved them.
He has always done special things for you,
And you have showed how much you loved Him.

Ron Brown

Family and friends are part of His plan
And a few special people are too.
He showers you daily with His blessings,
And He does it just for you.

Our faith in the Lord should remain strong;
Our trust in Him shall not waver.
One of these days we will sing a new song
And shall be with the Lord forever.

Christmas Time

Christmas Time is the time of good cheer,
With lots of memories of the past years.
But this will be the first Christmas I will be without her;
I will miss her smile and getting to hear her laughter.

Over fifty years she was always by my side,
Now her spirit is in Heaven, where she now abides.
The memories of the Christmas with our first child,
Are very rewarding but a little bit mild.

When the second child came along we were filled with joy,
Our family was complete; we had a girl and a boy.
God gave us these gifts to love and raise
And at Christmas, we made sure to give Him praise.

At Christmas time our families always got together,
To celebrate the season, and hope for good weather.
We would alternate families every other year;
Everyone got to see us, whether far or near.

How Mom and Dad could stand all the noise,
When, we all got together, with our little girls and boys.
Everyone has gotten older; the children are now grown;
The children are now married and have families of their own.

Now, we know how Mom and Dad felt when we came home.
It was a glad reunion, and it felt so good, to be home.
The laughter and joy that often filled our hearts,
Would become saddened when one of us departs.

God called my wife Home, and in these past years,
It caused lots of pain, sorrow, and many tears.
He has filled our broken hearts with His peace;
His everlasting love for us will never cease.

God gave us a gift, the earthly birth of His Son.
When we believe in Him, our life has just begun.
Life without her will be different that's for sure,
But she is safe in the arms, of Him that is pure.

She'll not be across the table looking at me,
Or help put Christmas lights on our tree.
Just thinking what God gave to us over the years,
Brings happiness to me but also tears.

Christmas will never be the same now,
But with God's love, I'll make it somehow.
Just to know I will see our loved ones again,
In Heaven with Jesus, where it all began.

Old-Time Camp Meetings

I can remember the old camp meetings,
When the big main tent was pitched.
Next was a much smaller cook tent;
It was where all the meals were fixed.

Lots of people set up their own tents;
They couldn't wait for the services to begin.
Some people drove for many a mile, and
They would never know when a service would end.

As a boy, in business for myself,
I shined many a dusty shoe.
When the dinner bell rang or services began,
My shoe shining time was through.

Sometimes it was cool, many times it was hot.
A rainstorm would sometimes blow through,
But it never dampened our spirits because
The fresh air seemed to make everything new.

The choirs and singers that sang of His story,
You could hear from anywhere on the grounds.
Then the preachers began to tell of His glory;
How Jesus Christ could be sought and found.

God was there in our midst each and every day
And someone was prayed for and healed.
Afternoon services were always held
About an hour or so, after the noontime meal.

The straw that was spread around the altars,
Would be where many souls were saved.
The Lord forgave them of their sins as
They knelt before Him and prayed.

Just remembering these things makes my heart glad,
That in a place called camp meeting time,
You will meet the best friend you've ever had—
A friend called Jesus that is with you all the time.

Give thanks to the Lord for camp meeting nights,
But don't forget the hot summer days.
He will send his blessings out to us daily
And He will do it in so many ways.

> This is the day that the Lord hath made;
> We will rejoice and be glad in it.

Psalm 118:24

The Fifty-First Anniversary

Celebrating our fifty-first anniversary
Without her, it was not a lot of fun.
As we celebrated our fiftieth,
The sickness had begun.

You see, I lost my loved one;
Cancer has taken her life.
Almost fifty-one years ago,
This grand lady became my wife.

The sickness that would take her life
Never was shown until it was too late.
The doctors told us of the curse
That would seal my loved one's fate.

Many prayers were given by people,
To our Heavenly Father above;
God had called our loved one's name;
He sent to us, His Comforter and love.

Everyone that ever met her,
She greeted with her smile.
If someone ever needed her help,
She would go that extra mile.

I thank God that He chose her
To be my mate; she was the love of my life.
She loved her family and her friends—
This wonderful lady that was my wife.

Though the smile she gave is now gone,
Lots of memories will still be there.
The Mother of my children
Had lots of God's love to share.

The Lord has eased our sorrow and
Helped take away all of our pain.
God will always be there for us, and
We shall look for His Heavenly Reign.

Part Seven: Special Days and Special People

SPECIAL
DAYS
AND
SPECIAL
PEOPLE

Mother's Day Without Mom

The first Mother's Day without her...
You wonder if you can make it through.
There were so many things you wanted to say
Before God called her away from you.

Through the many things she did for you
And the smiles she always made,
She always knew that you loved her,
And the memories of her will never fade.

She was a beautiful wife and terrific Mom.
Her family meant the world to her,
But God knew what was ahead of us,
And He knew of the sadness it would stir.

The pain she endured and still could smile,
Let us know she was ready to leave.
She had seen what God had planned for her.
We had all prayed, and she believed.

Ron Brown

I know she is looking down on us
To see what we will do.
The first Mother's Day without her,
She will be sure we make it through.

There are plenty of Mothers that are alone
And don't have anyone left to love,
So find a Mother that needs your help
And give her all your love.

Your wife and your children's Mother
Will be pleased at what you do.
Just remember the joys that you have shared
And that she and God still love you.

Heavenly Father's Day

To our Father that is in Heaven,
We send this praise to You.
We wish You to have a terrific day,
And our earthly fathers too.

We thank You for our Christian fathers,
That prayed to You each day;
Our Christian mothers knelt beside them,
As they asked You to lead their way.

We thank You for a Christian family,
That was completely devoted to You.
Though there were many troubles and trials,
You would always see them through.

You have provided us with many things…
More than our earthly fathers can give,
And when we have a Christian father,
It influences the way we live.

Ron Brown

Lord, we honor You on this Father's Day,
By devoting our lives to You.
May we live according to Your Holy Word,
The way You would want us to.

Dear Father, pour down Your blessings on us;
May we drink of Your living water.
May we always give thanks for what we have.
With Heaven in sight, that's all that matters.

Grandmothers

When God blesses you with a precious gift,
He trusts you with this bundle of joy.
This small little person that you call your own,
Will melt your heart, whether it is a girl or boy.

Along with this birth, comes another person;
One with the experience you can rely on.
She has many names and does many things.
This is the time when a Grandmother is born.

She has spent sleepless nights wondering,
What her grandchild will be like?
When the time comes for its arrival,
Will she be ready for this little tyke?

She is as excited as the parents are,
About this new addition to her family.
She can't wait to hold it in her arms,
And to watch it laugh, while bouncing on her knee.

Nana, Grammy, Granny, Grandma, Grandmother—
She answers to them all and always has open arms.
When she lives miles away she can't stand to leave;
She will miss her grandchild and all of its charms.

She is always ready to talk about her grandchild,
And always has pictures to show.
Just mention to her about going to see them,
And she is always ready to go.

God sometimes calls a Grandmother to heaven,
Before a grandchild is grown.
It's hard for the little ones to understand,
Why God has called for His own.

She prayed many times for her family,
"God please keep your loving hand on them."
Now she is in Heaven and knows…
All her prayers were answered by Him

God blesses families with Grandmas that pray;
Be thankful for the blessings He gives.
Grandmas that take time for a prayer,
Shows you exactly how she lives.

Her grandchild may be her pot of gold,
But the love for her God is greater.
Her faith is building treasures in Heaven,
Because she believes in God, the Creator.

> Blessed are the pure in heart, for they
> Shall see God.

Matthew 5:8

Thanksgiving

To some people, Thanksgiving is just a day in a year when you have turkey and all the fixins' and your family or some close friends are with you. Thanksgiving to a Christian is more than that. It is thanks for life and the future it holds.

It is a time to praise the Lord for all of the things He has done for you. His everlasting compassion and love for us will never cease. He has filled our hearts with joy, because we know, one of these days we will see our loved ones who have gone before us. We shall be rid of all temptations that the Evil One throws at us, and shall get to look upon the face of Jesus.

I give thanks for the wonderful wife that the Lord gave me. Through the fifty-plus years we were married, He never once left our side. We, on the other hand, strayed from Him. He was always there for us, even though we failed to acknowledge Him.

He gave us two gifts of life: a daughter and a son. He trusted us enough to raise them and teach them right from wrong and to always give him the praise and the glory He deserved. Although we failed to always follow His lead, He, somehow forgave us and helped keep us on the right path. When trials came our way, it wasn't us that solved them, but God Almighty. When loved ones were lost, He felt our sorrow and gave us peace.

This is my prayer of thanks:

I thank the Lord for my sight that
I may see the beauty that surrounds me.
I thank the Lord for the family he gave me.
I thank the Lord for my sense of feeling so that
I can feel the warmth of love from my family.
I thank the Lord for His forgiveness of my sins.
I thank the Lord for His unshakable love
He has for me.
I thank God for giving His only Son,
To die on the cross for me.
I thank the Lord for giving me a chance
Of an Eternal Life; it's up to me to fulfill it.
I thank the Lord for being the same yesterday,
 Today and forever.

AMEN

Giving thanks always for all things unto God
And the Father in the name of our Lord Jesus Christ.

Ephesians 5:20

LaFon

I knew this sweet lady for over fifty years—
This sweet lady, that became my wife.
I gave to her my heart one day;
She has been the love of my life.

God gave gifts of two children for us to love;
He now had made our family complete.
And we knew that as we raised them,
We could leave all our cares at His feet.

This lady was so gentle and kind,
And everyone was a friend.
LaFon loved her family and her God,
And was true to them until the end.

Her pleasant voice and welcoming smile
Greeted people every day.
She loved her work and the people she met,
Now God has called her away.

Life without LaFon will be very tough;
The tears will often be shed.
When I remember those yesterday years,
I can hear her say "With this ring I thee wed."

Now all that's left is fond memories,
For my children, and for me.
Through the joys and sorrows that we shared,
We knew that God had blessed our family.

God called LaFon from the family she loved;
No matter how hard we prayed.
We prayed for healing from above,
But it wasn't the plans God had made.

The family has trusted in God's great plan;
We know she's in Heaven with Him.
One of these days we will get to see her again,
When God calls us, to be with Him.

I give God the glory for LaFon's earthly life
And the eternal life she now wears.
Christ gave His blood on the cross for us.
We as believers, become Heaven's Heirs.

> He that finds a wife finds a good thing and
> Obtains favor from the Lord.

Proverbs 18:22

The Preacher Man

A few days ago, a special friend was called away
From his family and friends, that he loved.
Now he rests in the arms of his Savior,
At God's Kingdom in the Heavens above.

He strummed his guitar, sang praises to the Lord,
And spread God's Word over the countryside.
He was doing what he loved to do most;
He was doing God's will when he died.

His life was full of the love of God,
And he gave freely of his time.
But heartache and trauma had taken its toll,
When suddenly his wife died, before her time.

He traveled around preaching God's word…
Strumming on his guitar as he spoke.
He was devoted to telling Christ's story
To the businessman or the cowpoke.

His style of preaching will be missed
From South Texas to the Great Plains.
He taught young believers in Bible School,
That knowing God, they had everything to gain.

Family and friends will miss this man;
His life had a "laid-back" style.
He seemed to never have a worry, because
Everywhere he went, he always wore a smile.

Now he is at forever peace in Heaven,
With friends and loved ones up there.
One great day we will see him again,
When all believers meet Jesus, in the air.

"Go into all the world and preach the Gospel
To every creature."

Mark 16:15

My Daughter

There was a reason that God sent you—
The first child of your Mom and I.
He knew how long our marriage would last,
And which of us would be the first to die.

Tremendous joy filled our hearts,
On the day you arrived.
God had given us a great gift;
He gave us a daughter to enrich our lives.

He knew that when I looked at you,
I could see your Mom's reflection...
From the smile that she always had,
To even the same beautiful complexion.

He gave you the same personality,
That was seen in your Mom's life.
He knew that she would be a perfect Mom,
So He picked her to be my wife.

You have always been kind of a tomboy.
You helped me do things around the house.
There are not many things you could not do,
But you just couldn't kill a mouse.

You have a stubborn streak in you,
That had to come from me.
Sometimes to get you to mind us,
We got a switch from a tree.

You never meet a stranger,
Just like your Mom used to be.
That's why I love you so much;
You mirror your Mom to me.

Although you suffer from many ills,
You still can manage a big smile.
It tells me that you love me,
But you still need to rest for a while.

God knows your troubles and trials;
He has seen your jubilant days.
God knows how much you miss your Mom;
How you remember her in so many ways.

God helped ease your sorrow,
When He provided you with a second Mom.
Aunt Fern stepped in to take her place;
She was happy to act as your Mom.

Because of the CROSS

The compassion you have for God's critters
Seems to let them know you are a friend.
I have seen the trust they put in you;
May your love for them never end.

Just like God has compassion for us,
He will always be our friend and Savior.
We must trust Him in everything we do,
And His love for us will not waver.

Many years have gone by,
Since that day you entered our world.
I want you to know I love you,
And you are still my little girl.

Part Eight: He Is the Reason

HE
IS THE
REASON

Do You Know the Reason?

Many people overlook the reason
That we celebrate this time of the year.
They are more interested in gifts and family
And doing lots of things of good cheer.

People have forgotten to teach their children
About Jesus and His miraculous birth.
There was a very specific reason
That He was sent from Heaven to earth.

God's only Son was given to people here on earth.
It was and is the greatest gift ever,
When we celebrate Jesus's birth,
It also shows God's love for us, is forever,

Not much is known about Christ's younger years;
He probably acted like a normal boy.
He would always pay attention to his parents,
And helped his Dad, especially when making toys.

Ron Brown

But He soon began His work in earnest:
It was the reason He came down to earth.
Lots of prophets spoke of this reason,
Many years before His birth.

Christ chose a few men to follow Him,
As He went about teaching God's word.
He prayed for the sick and healed the lame,
And there was never a discouraging word.

But the real reason we should celebrate,
Is not the birth of Jesus, our Savior?
It is because He died on the cross for us,
And when we believe in Him, we have God's favor.

Christ became the sacrifice for our sins;
It was his sole purpose here on earth.
We have the promise of eternal life,
And it all started with His birth.

Because of the CROSS

We all look forward to Christmas Day,
When we have fun with family and friends,
But we must not lose sight of Jesus,
And His love that is with us to the end.

So as we gather together today,
We thank You Father for what You have done.
You gave us the gifts of mercy and love,
When you sent to us, Your Son.

Christmas

While most of the world is waiting for Christmas
With Santa Claus and all the presents,
The Christian is also waiting for Christmas,
To honor our Lord and stand in His Presence.

The Virgin Mary gave birth to a Son...
The Son of the Father from above.
Our Lord and Savior had been born...
A present from God, with all His love.

The Heavenly angels sang at His birth,
"Peace on earth and goodwill to man."
Kings came from afar to honor His birth,
As word of His birth spread over the land.

We had received to man, the greatest gift ever,
But few failed to believe He was the Son of God.
They said He just couldn't be the promised one
And refused His claim to be the Son of God.

The evil one tried to persuade Him
With all kinds of promises we are told.
Jesus rebuked the evil one and his words,
And soon His ministry began to unfold.

Because of the CROSS

He traveled by foot over many miles.
With his disciples, He covered the land.
The sick were healed and lame made whole,
With His word or by the touch of His hand.

He preached the word to all that would listen;
Big crowds were fed by His prayer to the Father.
He calmed the seas, made the dead come to life,
And He blessed the believers' sons and daughters.

His life here on earth was very short,
But what an impact it has made;
His life has been told for many years,
And never will His word ever fade.

He suffered pain we should never forget,
When He died on Calvary's Tree.
He died of a broken heart that day,
But He did it for you and me.

His life touched everyone He met,
And still does to this very day;
The story of His life here on earth
Makes the Bible the best seller today.

So let us not forget why we have Christmas,
God's gift to us was forever;
From a babe in a manger to a man of peace,
It was and is the greatest gift ever.

So, when we give gifts at Christmas time,
We are remembering Jesus's birth.
The gift God gave was just one of His gifts
When He sent His Son to earth.

The Small Barn

On the outskirts of a village, sits a small barn...
Holes in the walls, not much of a roof, and no doors at all.
It has a dirt floor covered with a little straw,
And has the smell of animals, standing in their stall.

Things were about to happen, when a man and his wife,
Found only this barn, to stay the night.
Soon there was a great light shining from above;
It was coming from a single star that shined so bright.

The man and his wife had traveled many miles;
Their clothes were dusty and their feet were tired.
They had come to pay taxes to Caesar, but
All the Inns were full, so this was the last place they tried.

The man and his wife began using straw to make a bed;
The husband held her hand as he made them, a light.
The woman was with child and she began to moan,
She knew now, that this would be the night.

God had told the woman
That she would deliver a Son—
The Son of God who would rule the world and
Would be the Messiah and Savior of everyone.

A small cry was heard—the child had been born!
The man covered the child and laid it in the manger.
Just then a Shepherd showed up and blew on his horn,
The star became brighter over the barn and manger.

The light from the star was seen for many miles,
As more shepherds came to visit the child.
Kings came from afar guided by the light from the star;
They came to see this child, so tender and mild.

The small barn and the lowly manger that night,
Became the Temple of our Lord and King.
It glowed from the light of the star that night,
And all the angels sang and bells did ring.

Some people heard of the birth and were not pleased,
That another king had been born that night.
Angels told the man and his wife to flee from there,
And when they left the small barn, so did the light.

When we are born again into His Kingdom,
Our body becomes His Temple.
Just like the small barn, His light will shine on us;
The Word of God is very simple.

Because of the CROSS

When we give our hearts to God,
We keep His commandments and do what is right,
But like the small barn, when Christ is left out,
We will lose His favor and also lose the light.

Give glory to God for His everlasting love,
And the Son that He sent down from above.
Just remember Christ is the reason,
That we get together to celebrate the season.

Heavenly Party

Then the Angel of the Lord came to Mary and said,
"Soon you shall be the Mother of a King."
"How can that be?" she said. "I have not known a man;
I don't even wear a betrothal ring."
The Angel calmed Mary and assured her,
That everything would be alright.
God had planted a special seed in her,
And the world would soon have a new Light.

When Mary told Joseph what had happened to her,
He pondered on what he should do.
In a vision to Joseph, in the night,
God began to show him what he was to do.
Joseph took Mary to be his lovely wife,
With no doubts and no fear;
It was a marriage planned by God,
And He promised that He would be near.

Soon it was time to pay the tax man;
A trip to Jerusalem they both would take.
The trip wasn't easy for Mary,
But she knew it was a trip she had to make.
Arriving sometime after sunset,
No rooms were found at the inns.

Because of the CROSS

A lowly stable was all they could find,
When Mary's labor pains would begin.

The Angels appeared and began to sing,
When Baby Jesus was born.
They have continued to this day,
And are still tooting their horns.
What a party they had in Heaven;
The Angels started spreading the word.
A huge Angelic chorus sang new songs
That never before were heard.

The Star shone bright, and the Angels sang,
As our Lord and Savior was born!
Because of Him, we have eternal hope,
And from Satan's grip we are torn.
The gift that God gave to us that day,
Was His one and only Son.
It showed what true love really is,
Because that's when our salvation begun.

> And she shall bring forth a son, and thou
> Shalt call his name JESUS: for he shall
> Save his people from their sins.

Matthew 1:21

What Does Christmas Mean to You?

Christmas time in our world today,
Can mean many things to lots of people.
To some it means time with loved ones,
And attending services at the church with a steeple.

To others it means vacation time,
And travel to all sorts of places.
Others get enjoyment from giving gifts,
And seeing the smiles on others' faces.

To small children it is a time of joy,
Because of all the presents they will be receiving.
To adults it is a time of joy and celebration,
Because of the gifts they will be giving.

To all Christians, it is a time of remembering
The greatest gift the world has ever received,
The birth of a King to God's Heavenly Kingdom,
And eternal life for all, that have believed.

Because of the CROSS

Christmas means that God loved you,
And He gave to us a treasure.
The Son that He loved, and sent to earth,
With mercy and grace, no man can measure.

He gave His best to save the least,
From sin and all that it holds.
His son died on the cross just for us,
So we can see Heaven and all it holds.

So remember the Christ Child at Christmas,
And all the gifts that came with Him.
Also, remember that He died on the cross,
So we could be in Heaven with Him.

> And the angel said unto her, "Fear not, Mary:
> For thou hast found favor with God.
> And, behold thou shalt conceive in thy womb,
> And bring forth a son and shalt call his name
> JESUS."

Luke 1:30,31

Part Nine: That's All

THAT'S
ALL
THE END IS NEAR

The Warnings

When our Nation was founded,
In God we put our trust.
He put a hedge of protection about us,
And everything we did was just.

Our forefathers put God in all of our laws,
But our high courts read it a different way.
We have become a nation without God,
And now we have a price to pay.

We wonder why violence is growing in our nation,
And particularly in our schools,
Why our country is in such disarray,
And why it is being run by a bunch of fools?

The hedge of protection has been breached;
God's anger is beginning to show.
We have forgotten what has been preached
About the God our nation does not know.

The first warning came from God
In September, two thousand and one.
Our nation drew back to the church and God,
But in a little while, our worshipping was done.

We said we will be strong and rebuild;
We didn't include God in our pledge.
Our nation is so self-reliant and strong,
So to prove His point, He removed the hedge.

As long as we keep trusting in ourselves
And ignore the God, who is our protector,
The harbingers tell us of each warning,
And the storms will come in different sectors.

Each natural storm occurrence will rain havoc.
All violence and destruction will be greater,
Until we return to the Heavenly Father,
Our protector and creator.

We are following the steps of Israel
As found in Isaiah chapter nine, verse ten.
We are not heeding God's words now,
And Israel didn't heed them back then.

America has received her warnings.
The harbingers have been sounded.
We need to get back into God's grace
And be the nation we were when founded.

Because of the CROSS

Our nation has sinned greatly.
Her destruction will be great!
Because we have kept God out of our lives,
We as a nation have sealed our fate.

So we can look forward to our nation
Being racked with suffering and pain.
Until our leaders realize what has happened
And return to worship our Lord once again.

America the Beautiful, Once Again

I've been praying and talking to the Lord,
About the things that are happening down here.
How the power of America has begun to fade,
And its joy has turned to fear.

Our nation has strayed too far from Him,
In everything we say or do.
Lord I pray to you on this day,
And this is what He said to do.

"America the beautiful, can be once again,
But this is the only way it can be.
You must stop worshipping all of your idols,
And begin calling once again on Me."

"You need to put prayer back into the schools;
Put my commandments back on the wall.
When you took all of this away from Me,
Is when America began its fall."

"Domestic violence will begin to increase;
Storms will begin to pummel the land.
Things like this will never end,
Until on Me you will make a stand."

Because of the CROSS

"America the beautiful, can be once again,
But this is the only way it can be.
You must stop worshipping all of your idols,
And begin calling once again on Me."

"My hedge of protection I will restore for you,
If you would just call on My name.
The book I have written and you have in your hand,
Remind you, that I will always be the same."

"So wake up, America, if you want things to change,
You better start listening to Me.
Give up your way of a sinful life,
And get back to worshipping Me."

"America the beautiful, can be once again,
But this is the only way it can be.
You must stop worshipping all of your idols,
And began praying once again to Me."

> "Return to Me, and I will return to you,"
> Says the Lord of Hosts.

Malachi 3:7

What Would You Do?

If during your nighttime dreams,
God would give you a vision.
You were told to get your life in order;
What would be your most important decision?

Would you thank Him for the life you have had,
And pray for the family you leave behind?
Would you wish that you had helped the poor often,
And had been more considerate and kind?

Would you ask God to bless your family,
And guard them against all pitfalls?
Have you been faithful to the Lord?
Have you given Him your all?

Are there things you have done lately,
That you need to ask forgiveness for?
Have you had road rage, judged someone,
Or repeated gossip you heard at the store?

Because of the CROSS

When you looked back on your life,
Was it free from trials and tribulations?
Did you praise God during the hard times,
Or only when you were filled with jubilation?

Would you begin to study His word more?
Would you thank Him for everything, everyday?
Would you begin to show more compassion for others?
Would you ask for His guidance, in your
Remaining days?

Would you start thinking what will happen
To all your loved ones, and your possessions?
Would you start collecting debts owed to you?
Are you filled too much with earthly obsessions?

Are your earthly treasures so valuable
That you must get everything you seek?
Do You feel like you have done God's will,
By honoring Him once a week?

You have donated money to His service
But have you donated your time?
Have you visited with the sick,
Or, with someone in jail, for a crime?

Ron Brown

There are rewards in Heaven for believers;
The size depends on what you did down here.
Good deeds alone will not save you,
But by the mercy of the God we fear.

Have you given your heart and soul to the Lord,
So you may have an eternal life with Him?
Or have you rejected His call too many times,
And the devil will have you in the lake of fire,
With him.

What really would you do,
If God said your earthly life is through?
It would make you stop and think.
It does me, how about you?

The End and Beginning

I have come to the end of my journey;
No more am I able to roam.
I have found a place that's out of this world;
I now call Heaven my home.

The Son of God that died on the cross,
Shed His blood so that from sin I was made free.
Because of His abundance of love for me,
The victory in Jesus, I now see.

My life has been full of blessings and joy,
But sometimes the storms of sorrow were there.
God keeps His promises; He was with me through the storms,
And as a believer, I am one of His Heavenly heirs.

The Lord of mercy and love unending
Chose me to be one of His own.
Now I am on my way to Heaven
To see my Jesus on His throne.

I know my family will miss me;
I am going to a better place.
I pray that God will be with them
And give them peace and comfort in my place.

Give praise and glory to our Lord;
He is The One who gave us His Son.
A Son that suffered and died on the cross,
In a fight against sin, and He won!

I now begin a new life in Heaven;
What a glorious place it will be.
A life that will be indescribable,
And Jesus made it possible for me.